The Sun

by Martha E. H. Rustad

raintree

a Capstone company — publishers for children

Raintree is an imprint of Capstone Global Library Limited, a company incorporated in England and Wales having its registered office at 264 Banbury Road, Oxford, OX2 7DY – Registered company number: 6695582

www.raintree.co.uk
myorders@raintree.co.uk

Edited by Erika L. Shores
Designed by Juliette Peters and Katelin Plekkenpol
Picture research by Tracy Cummins
Production by Katy LaVigne
Originated by Capstone Global Library
Printed and bound in China.

ISBN 978 1 4747 1252 1

19 18 17 16 15
10 9 8 7 6 5 4 3 2 1

British Library Cataloguing in Publication Data
A full catalogue record for this book is available from the British Library.

Acknowledgements
We would like to thank the following for permission to reproduce photographs:
Getty Images: Juice Images, 5; Science Source: Eric Cohen, 13, Mark Garlick, 9; Shutterstock: Kalenik Hanna, Design Element, lassedesignen, 19, Mopic, 15, Paul Fleet, 17, PaulPaladin, 11, Triff, Cover, 1, 7, Zurijeta, 21.

Every effort has been made to contact copyright holders of material reproduced in this book. Any omissions will be rectified in subsequent printings if notice is given to the publisher.

All the internet addresses (URLs) given in this book were valid at the time of going to press. However, due to the dynamic nature of the internet, some addresses may have changed, or sites may have changed or ceased to exist since publication. While the author and publisher regret any inconvenience this may cause readers, no responsibility for any such changes can be accepted by either the author or the publisher.

Editor's Note
In this book's photographs, the sizes of objects and the distances between them are not to scale.

Contents

About the Sun

The Sun shines.

Feel its heat.

See its light.

What is the Sun?

A star!

Stars are balls

of burning gases.

The Sun's place

The Sun sits in the Milky Way. Our galaxy looks like a disc.

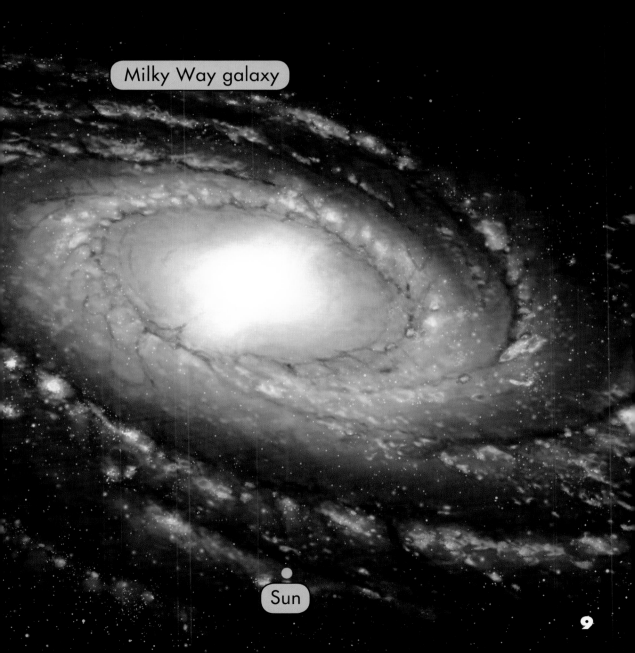

Milky Way galaxy

Sun

How far away is the Sun?
About 150 million kilometres
(93 million miles)!

Big and hot

The Sun is huge.

It is as wide as 109 Earths.

Earth

Sun

Inside the Sun is the core.

The Sun is hottest there.

core

Solar flares shoot out.

Hot gases escape.

The Sun and Earth

The Sun always shines.

Earth turns. Our side faces

the Sun. It is day.

Our side turns away.

It is night.

19

We need the Sun.

Its heat warms Earth.

Its rays light Earth.

Thank you, Sun!

Glossary

galaxy   large group of billions of stars

gas   substance that spreads to fill any space that holds it

planet   large object in space that orbits a star

ray   line of light and heat

solar flare   burst of energy and gas from the Sun's surface

star   ball of burning gases; the Sun is a star

Find out more

Sun, Moon and Stars (Kingfisher Readers), Hannah Wilson (Kingfisher, 2014)

The Sun (Space). Charlotte Guillain (Raintree, 2010)

Websites

solarsystem.nasa.gov/planets/profile.cfm?Object=Sun
Learn facts about the Sun on this website.

www.spacecentre.co.uk
Visit the National Space Centre in Leicester.

Index